# THE MANY FACES OF MARIAMA

## The Fourth Letter

by
**Rhythma of De'twa**

## The Many Faces of Mariama
## by
## Rhythma of De'twa

Cover designed
by
Donele "Casino" Bailey

Published by Mocy Publishing, LLC
Copyright © 2011 by Jeana Tall. All rights reserved. Except as permitted under the United States Copyright Act of 1976, no part of this publication may be reproduced or distributed in any form or by any means, or stored in a data base or retrieval system, without the prior written permission of the publisher. This book is also available in print at most of your book retail stores.

**Discover other titles
by
Rhythma of De'twa
at Mocybox.com**

# The Many Faces of Mariama – The Fourth Letter

**Table of Contents**

The Many Faces of Mariama............5
Losing the War............7
Hello?............9
Carpet Burn............10
Speaking Freely............12
Dear Etienne'............13
Brutha Man............14
Reach............16
I Miss Yah............18
The Real............20
Dead Love............21
My Name............22
Killing Me............23
To Live............24
Spring Healing............26
My Permanent Tan............27
Fear............28
As Cruel............30
Take Care............32
Peek-a-Boo............34
Rock This Party............36
Wad Up Dough?............37
Love Myself............38
Grown and Sexy............40
Microwave............41
Sistah Need a New Pair Shoes............42
I Put my Life on the Line............43
The King's Ball............44
We Got Bigger Fish to Fry............45
Let Me In Your Soul............46
A Million Dollars............47
Do You Think About Me............48

## The Many Faces of Mariama – The Fourth Letter

| | |
|---|---|
| Why? | 49 |
| Our Watchman | 50 |
| Stand | 51 |
| You Ain't Cool | 52 |
| EM | 53 |
| Time | 54 |
| When I Fell in Love With You | 59 |
| Hitched | 61 |
| What? | 63 |
| 360 Degrees | 64 |
| Sugar Daddy | 66 |
| Gotta Keep On Moving | 68 |
| I Need You Baby | 69 |
| Could I Just Love You For Awhile? | 71 |
| Stand Again | 73 |
| Endangered Species | 74 |
| Want to Believe | 75 |
| I Got Naps | 77 |
| 2 Lives | 78 |
| Not Even a Glimpse of Love | 79 |
| When We Write History | 80 |
| I Am Found Where Love Is | 81 |
| Got To Be Strong | 83 |
| Never Told Me Why | 84 |
| A Poem to the Africans Born In America | 85 |

## The Many Faces of Mariama

The search continues
as the blues and rhythm
find me in them.
I send wind chimes
on Nursery Rhymes
and roller coaster rides
that challenges your screams.
Imagination to challenge your dreams.
Yet and still I find myself losing my will
to find myself.

With each thought of inquiry
I discover mentally that my depth is
deep and my existence wide
and so myself finds infinite
dimensions to hide.

As I touch upon or uncover
alas, another is discovered.
With dreams and manifestations
unlike the others.

What shall become of me?
when me is two and sometimes three?
And,
I am never satisfied to limitations
or abide by laws of society or
silly boundaries.

Life brings much more pleasure
when I can measure, treasures
with many eyes and mouths

# The Many Faces of Mariama – The Fourth Letter

to taste.

What a waste to settle where
the others fear and never care
to live more than one life
in its duration instead
they point a finger, hating me.

Blaming me for living life
to its fullest capacity.
Never wanting to understand me.
Just mad cause they can't use me.

Cause sometimes me is two or three.

These many faces of Mariama
bring joy and sadness with plenty drama.
Living a stage and writing a play
is my every day.
No one can fault me for the excitement
because I choose to be enlightened.
I create and create and create.

Until I've extracted rejuvenation
from my core or maybe more brain power
than the norm.

Whatever the formula, it's rarely duplicated
so that I seem to have created
a phenomenal creation within me.

As they see, sometimes me is two or three.

# The Many Faces of Mariama – The Fourth Letter

## Losing the War

We are losing the war.
But the war is in your heads.
You will not infect or inject
my sons with your filth, your filthy sin.
That is my flesh and my blood
you disregard as mud.
Flood my eyes with tears and fears
of losing his sweet flesh to your street mess.
Cell blocks at the age of 9,
seeing daylight at 79.
Now who is really doing the crime and
who is doing the time, it is I.
And I didn't want to be your fool.
So, I ask you,
can you please let my son graduate from high school
without a bullet in his chest.
You got me standing over my son,
saying rest in peace
but there is no peace on the streets of the D.
Because you believe in an eye for an eye
and a tooth for a tooth.
Now we both bury our young and we both bury our youth.
Now what more is there for us to do?
Because ever since we came over here on those boats
you aint' never wanted to let us go.
You love us so much, you locked up our dough.
Our dough is the black man and the black man is our dough.
And then you knock on my doe (door),
And I say, he don't live here no moe (more).
Cause he is locked up, shot up or cocked up.
And now I wear the pants

and I cock the 9 at the doe (door).
But we are tired though.
Tired of the cell blocks that spell black they call crack
And Shaka Senghor said, you can't take none of those years back.
We are losing the war
because you locked up our protector.
But the war is in your heads
and it is making you leave your people for dead.

**Hello?**

Ring, Ring,
Hello?
Hello.
I was just about to shoot myself in the head.
Call me back when I am dead.
Click.

## Carpet Burn

Carpet burn,
still fresh
on my
yearning
flesh.
Burning skin
churning within.
Your love
has made a scar
so bizarre
within
my heart
emotional
roller coaster
ride
now I'm tough
like cowhide.
Never
dry eyed
they stare
concerned
bout my carpet
burn.
Visible for
all to see
A poster board
of my
sexuality.
The ride
was rough
sand paper
tough.

## The Many Faces of Mariama – The Fourth Letter

It smoothed
the surface
I curse
this scar
so bizarre
and yet
I yearn
for your love
carpet
burn.

## Speaking Freely

You couldn't walk a mile in my shoes.
High and mighty, you would fall,
flat on your face trying to ball,
trying to be all that you can be
in this fucked up, hypocritical country.

You couldn't sing the blues that I've sang.
Mad as hell, in the rain, pissed off cause
you trying to rip my pride off.

People, quit trying to define a sistah
when what you're really thinkin
is, "Damn, I miss her and I wish her
next move would be next to me, so
maybe some of that creativity
will rub off on me and I can stop
sittin here, like I'm just part of the
atmosphere."

Don't think that you know me
cause you don't.
Except you wish that you could be me,
you hear that?
That is the sound of the aroma
of love,
something you don't of
something you don't know nothin
bout since you played yourself out
trying to play me,
I'm just speaking freely.

## The Many Faces of Mariama – The Fourth Letter

### **Dear Etienne'**

How close could we be
without being the same
having the same name
wearing the same clothes?
I know that you are a part of me
like another leg or arm or an eye
or a heart right from the start.
I knew that it would be me and you
and they couldn't separate us.
We try and live as individuals
it's incredible how are lives are
parallel.
No one could tell if years or months
go by, we say"Hi" as if it hadn't.
It makes me sad that you aren't here.
A true sad that brings fear to my heart.
That lets me know a part of me is missing.
I'm wishing I could talk to you and
no one else right at this moment.
I need to hear you laugh and
tell me I don't understand math.
Tell me I'll be all right cause you know
there is something in my voice that just
isn't quite right and you know when
no one else does what it was I wanted
to say.
And now I want to say that no matter
who becomes your foe, enemy or friend,
no matter how small or big, the entity,
I claim you as a part of me.

## Brutha Man

Brutha man,
understand I am
by your side
on this roller coaster ride
you got me on.
Though our love is strong,
do you realize the bond
that ties us like ribbons or knots?
Have we forgot the years
of dedication to this love
cause you are my soul mate and
I can relate to your pain and the
fact that I got your back
should bring you comfort in your zone
plus,
I can't seem to leave you alone.

Brutha man,
I demand that your body be
in ecstasy. It is my destiny
to be your fantasy.
To bring your lips to fulfillment
like no other woman could
compliment and my scent
will drive you insane as your
animal instinct would be to blame
for your prowness as
I am your prey.

Brutha man,
where is the day and night
when I can engulf you in my

## The Many Faces of Mariama – The Fourth Letter

femaleness and you would
be in love from my sweet caress?
It's going to be all right.
I will declare and let the public
stare as you make love to me
beyond compare
and I love you back if I would dare.
My personal goal
is to lick you bare.
Could this be sin
or lust or can I trust this love
within, Brutha man?
Would you allow me to come inside
you like you do me and let me bring
you ecstasy?

Brutha man,
I lay here naked with free love
so fearlessly
so take it so that we can make it
through hard times and make love
until we die.

**Reach**

But for the thorns
could you behold
my beauty in all of
it's sad glory.

I being
in forlorn detail
to gain composure
as I replay
and tell my story.

Love took hold and
brought confusion as
I sit in this
abstract institution.

We sometimes call fate
I met this soul mate
less circumstance or chance
I contemplate.

Should I love or not love
this man?
My heart reaches
for a quick response.

Like reaching for the
thornful rose
not caring bout
the thornful chance.

That one small prick

## The Many Faces of Mariama – The Fourth Letter

to my finger or one
sinister kick to my heart

could set me apart from
love or lonely.
If I could make
a choice if only.

I could make a decision
to reach for that love
manifested rose.

# The Many Faces of Mariama – The Fourth Letter

## I Miss Yah

Some lady said
I don't need no man
in my bed.
Heard another say
don't need no brother
in my head
playing games
to get him to come home.
Maybe its best
I live alone.
I'm prone to feel
like I'm numb.
Can't feel the hurt
when you act dumb
and want to lift
my skirt and flirt with my
Sistah.
That's why I miss yah.
Told me you would
flip my dough.
Just give me some moe (more)
till your next check.
Now you talking
out of the side of your neck.
I'm reflecting. Checkin
your style now it's lookin
kinda shady when
I felt like I was your lady.
Now I feel like I'm yo mama
with all this drama
going on trying to keep
our relationship strong.

# The Many Faces of Mariama – The Fourth Letter

You just trying to keep your
hard on. What's wrong
with this picture?
That's why I miss yah.
Don't want to be a moron magnet
I feel stagnate.
No real man to guide me
just trying to hide me on
Saturday Nights.
Don't want to fight
so I stay home tryin not
to pick up the phone
then it dawned on me that
you leave thinking
I'm gonna believe
you ain't seeing
somebody. Where is the
party that I can't come to
cause you got yo string
of hoes following you
around like a piper clown
and so I dissed yah
that's why I miss yah.

## The Real

When will our souls
meet again?
When will my soul
make yours overflow?
Our souls
met some time ago
and now they miss each other's
glow
below
the surface
of the know
is the feel
and the heart
although
I may know
the real
it's the feel
that shoots the dart
start the fire
move the desire
to make the happen
bring full
understandin
it's not the mind
but the real
that I feel.

## Dead Love

I've burned it...
cremated it
into ashes.
I would like to
scatter those ashes
in the sea
and hold a prayer vigil
for our love.
I wish I could hold
a memorial service
for this love.
I would say the
eulogy.
I would say
how wonderful our
love once was.
I would talk about
the happy times
and how you would
hold me until
I felt like I was you.
I would weep
and someone would
help me to my seat.
The people would
shake my hand and kiss my cheek
and tell me they understand.
Our love was a gift,
I would say,
sorry, it had to die,
I would say.

## My Name

You don't know my name
cause my name is game.
You call me, yet I don't hear
cause my name is fear.
You think you know
my ins and outs
but, you don't know my doubts.
You see my left side
and can't see my right.
You don't judge my days
but judge my nights.
Don't call my name,
my name is blame.
You adorn my exterior,
yet, your revelation
is that my past is inferior.
Anyway, what was the criteria?
Oh yeah, mainstream hysteria.
You mouthed the syllables
of my name.
I heard it faintly and
looked around to see
who you were talking to.
It was you.
You see your own reflection, electing
to believe your own truths
My name is mirror, mirror
on the wall.
You don't know me at all.
Don't call my name,
my name is shame.

## Killing Me

In cages,
rages and despicable
behavior, no savior
in sight. The nights
are long,
the apologies missing
but, I can see the blood
dripping
on hands unwashed
and feet unkissed.
I made a list
of things to do,
one of them
to deal with you
and your need
to watch your brother bleed.
Watch him crawl,
make him small,
watch him cry.
Your selfishness
made him die.
Looking at yourself,
you see love
you see hate
your world is small
you can't see it all.
You can't see the knife
the bullet
that you let free
also is killing me.

## To Live

Toilet paper is a luxury
and everything you thought you knew
is nothing what is seems.
I took a trip to a
far away land in my mind.
Now, you can't control me
loss control of me and
you're running out of time.
Resolutions but,
it's confusing
how they choosing
to adapt.
Matter fact,
they just make it
into a soup,
when there's just
bones left
it will do.
From the inside out
they live
less privileges
using more than
just five senses
they live.
I give
because I receive
a fulfilled need
for following suit
to do what it is that
you came here to do.
To live.
Being bipolar

# The Many Faces of Mariama – The Fourth Letter

for the sake of a dollar
never stooping too low
grabbing life by the collar.
They wanna keep it to a whisper
but I gotta hollah
this message to all those listening
from the Muslim, to the Jew, to the Christian
I'm losing my integrity
messing around hopelessly
a victim of your strategy
to push your pharmacy
inside of me.
My name is Ritalin
but they didn't mention then
bout this crazed conspiracy
that if you messed around with me
you get a lifetime dependency.
Something that they
failed to say to me
there's no such thing as
ADHD.
Just me trying to find myself
in a world that values
wealth over
my sanity
slowly trying
to kill me.
But, I know better
why I wrote this letter.
Gotta faster pen
than your
malicious sin.

## Spring Healing

I don't have any more tears
left for you.
The river flows with
your memory residue.
I'm through.
As my lips form to
say those words,
birds
chirp and flowers
bloom to reassure
me that life won't exhume
my dead soul.
Like a tulip in
the flowerbed that
tricks you in the fall
only to bring pedals
in the spring.
I will rise up
again and smile
through it all.
I can't conceive that
happy or joyous
day as winter sets
deep down in my soul
and my heart hibernates.

## The Many Faces of Mariama – The Fourth Letter

### **My Permanent Tan**

I've got a permanent tan
and damn,
I won't take not one
more bite
of that media hype.
Drummer...
play your drums for real...
so they can feel
what I'm here to manifest.
That my tan can't be
sold, commercialized
or undressed.
You can't hate me
and then buy me
like the town hall
slave block.
The Mandingo hocked
more shingles
than his masters mare
or plantation.
This creation can't
be advertised
in summer's eyes.
I've got a permanent tan
with a permanent curl.
Nothing you could buy
in your salon world.

## Fear

You have no place here.
Release me.
Bring peace to me,
myself.
Because what I was,
I am not today.
Fear,
you have no place here!
Here in my space!
My space is my hole
for me to control!
Fear
we will not allow
you to plow through
our fortress
abort this scheme
to take away our dreams.
Fear
you are not my friend.
You disguise yourself
in my people and make me
hate them.
You throw your facade
in front of God for the wisdom
my elders lent me.
Fear
You are a used-to-be
who has no position
Listen!
I'm telling you to vacate
the premises so, respect
I may have spots
and I may have blemishes

But,
I don't have you,
anymore.

## As Cruel

They say jealously
is
as cruel as the grave.
I feel brave
that no envy
like what you send me
could get
any colder or bolder.
They say with friends
like you,
I don't need enemies
to bring me to my knees
in prayer
like you do
when I feel like you
don't care.
Mama said,
watch your back,
baby,
cause maybe
somebody gonna put
a knife in it
build strife in it,
your life.
I say,
yeah,
I'll love
this friend
from a distance.
Don't wanna be a witness
to my own homicide
as our worlds collide

## The Many Faces of Mariama – The Fourth Letter

and she can't hide
her jealously
no more.
I used to
adore you
but something happened
to your mental.
I moved up and out
when you just moved about.
You still trying
to catch up?
Yup.
Don't hate me
because I'm
beautiful,
I say,
That's not
why I hate you,
you say.

# The Many Faces of Mariama – The Fourth Letter

**Take Care**

You bit my style.
I said it first.
You used to be clean
but now you curse.
No rhyme to your shit
now you sound like
a top 40 hit.
I swear
they tell you to
copyright so your
friends won't bite
But I know
you didn't flow like that
yesterday
and your new piece,
well,
let's just say
it sounds familiar
whatever happened
to baby Jane?
Well, you know what
most people do
she must have came
and left
is it lame
to think
you've lost your ink.
Your pen is still
moving but like stella
you ain't grooving
maybe you should

## The Many Faces of Mariama – The Fourth Letter

slow your role
and acknowledge
whose style you stole
that's bold
but soon it will surface
to the top
when using somebody else's
style and you flop
Stop
There's still love
and a lot of time
to find yourself again
and admit your crime
this little identity crisis
ain't nothing
and an apology
always suffices
so come back
down to earth
and be yourself
and stay off of
other people's turf
Take care.

## Peek-a-Boo

I can see you
behind that
Mary Kay.
Did you take your
Prozac, today?
Your wrinkles were
so defined last week
before you fancied
your collagen treat.
You cheat
us of your real self
by wearing your wealth
inside your boobs.
Trying to look
like video girls
on the tube.
I can see you
behind the plastic
and silicon elastic.
Didn't think you
would ever do anything
this drastic
because they told you,
you weren't beautiful.
I know you.
I see you driving
that Benz on credit.
You wouldn't let it
get to you.
That divorce
taught you
a course in

## The Many Faces of Mariama – The Fourth Letter

hair weave and color
therapy.
It's scaring me.
You look good,
though.
You hide yourself,
well.

## Rock This Party

We gonna rock this party out
We gonna make you feel the D
We gonna party like we don't sleep.

We gonna rock this party rock this party

You're gonna know what we're about
We gonna make you feel the beat
We gonna give the people what they need
You gonna ask somebody bout the 313

## Wad Up Dough?

He never promised me a picket fence
But' I'm relentless
in my pursuit of happiness
I'm Blessed
But I must confess
every time he comes around I get undressed
It's complex
and I get so stressed
cause when I first got with him
that's when I stop saying next
Told him to text me
like Kwame Kilpatrick
Text me all the love
you gonna do on the mattress
slip this
like they do in the video
let me give you something you
can hold on to but
you don't hear me though
gotta keep it
clean for the radio
take it slow
the Detroit flow
Toe to Toe
We don't dance
we lean like Fat Joe
All the people trying to get moe (more)
of this Detroit Style this
D flow
if you in the 313 say What Up Doe.

## Love Myself

You don't have to check on me
I'll be fine
I walked out that door
Have to stick to it
this time
but my crime
is loving you
more than I love myself
myself myself

You don't have to lie to me
or waste your time
don't believe anything that comes
out of your mouth
but my crime
is loving you
more than I love myself
myself myself

Over and over again, when will this rollercoaster end?
The up and down of this relationship interferes with my egotrip.
My ego said B is my other personality
if you get on the wrong track with me then you will me the bipolar disorderly.
Its longevity, still in the D, reigning supreme but the people didn't stop to visit me
the Detroit oracle of HP they all say this about me
but they scared of the Buda in the tongue of the land of the free.
Over and Over again.
When will this relationship end?

## The Many Faces of Mariama – The Fourth Letter

I don't even want to be your friend.
Cuz you don't give a damn about a damn thing.
You're mad because I stand here with my self esteem.
You couldn't even touch it in your wildest dreams.
And your childish schemes just got regulated by my team.
And it brings me joy to know
that I never have to see your face no more.
I said, I never have to see your face no more.

## Grown and Sexy

Looking for a grown and sexy
man in this town
who makes you feel like a woman
not a little girl
getting caught with her
panties down
make you wanna ride in his caddy
call him daddy
all the way downtown

## Microwave

Leave the money
up under the microwave
cause you know you aint' shit
you ain't coming home today
sisters been calling your phone all day
while you leave me home alone
you go out to play
Macaulay Kaulkin
at home
smacking those cheeks
that's what brothers wanna
do you out in those streets
I'm at the poetry cafe on those beats
when you chasin those sisters them
brothers chasin me

## Sistah Need a New Pair Shoes

Sister need a new pair of shoes
but the brother wanna flex
and give her the blues
like she aint' new
like she aint got glue
like she can't stick around
like she aint right now
but I got some real bad news
everything she do
she do it real true
put money in your pocket to
decorate you
put honey on the lips
to pow wow with you
put miles on the jet so
she don't crowd you
but when the crowd gets rowdy
they get loud and rude
But sistah need a new pair of shoes
so the brother wanna flex and give her the blues.

## I Put my Life on the Line

I put my life on the line for the truth
and if you can't accept it, I feel sorry for you.
I'm on the front line for the truth.
Cause I'm a soldier, what about you.
Their bullets are words with silver tip lies
I say what you won't, I write on the skies.
Write my words on my temple
and my heart on my sleeve
if the bullet penetrates me
the truth will bleed.
I will never concede,
I will never concede,
to the greed
cause that's a soldier's creed.

## The King's Ball

We don't say today, what's on our mind.
Instead we let fate make us appreciate.
That is not the way of the conscious man
who owns no cowardly bone
only selfless acts
with no repayment.
Don't wait for the eulogy
to bring your tears because
your fears overwhelm your shame
and so you blame time or
the lack thereof
when love is the tribute even the shameless
can't stand mute.
Come one, come all,
to this King's Ball.
Whose throne is in the trenches
where the beggars lie and
whose hands we don't shake
but make us shiver as we deliver bread.
Don't dread his suffering or his plight.
Just bring your tribute on this night.

## We Got Bigger Fish to Fry

And we came here to make this party live.
Yall been waiting for some time,
since Eminem first took you inside
the 313 Collective.
It's the 313 Collective
We all got a real important message
The whole world's been neglecting
So pay up we're here we're collecting.
Need to be collecting those checks
bread and chips
deposit slips.
Cash.
Money that make my name drop from bitches lips.
We want to take those trips
on yachts and jets
so we can flex
we decided we want to bling
like Gucci mane
it's time for each of you to know my name.
You trying to knock me off my throne
but where you trying to knock me to?
We a team chic
if you don't believe chic
you can't get behind me
no fresher female mc in line
rewind
no recession just a blessing
it's a power shift
pretty soon everybody will be
trying to get with this shit.

**Let Me In Your Soul**

Let me in your soul
I'll make you whole again
Let me take control
Wanna be your inspiration

Be my confidante
I'll talk to your pillow
Let me heal your heart
I understand your sorrow.

**A Million Dollars**

I see a million dollars
on the other side of that mountain
gonna take a sip of this fountain
and meet you on the other side.
Come take a ride to the other side

## Do You Think About Me

Do you think about me
when you're talking to her
Do you know how that hurts
when you're talkin to her
When she lays in your arms
and you give her your charms.
You give it all away
make me don't want to stay.
I want to sound the alarm.
Do you even know me?
Do you know what I need?
Take me off of your string
making me want to swing
every time your phone rings.
Did not want to cling
to a star
cuz I know who you really are.

## Why?

Why do you make me feel this way
Cuz I been there for you
Every time we're together
I get nothing but the blues.

## Our Watchman

Somebody gave us a watchman
Somebody gave us a king
and if you aint man enough to tell it.
I'll be the woman who truth brings
Somebody loves all his people cause.
They gave us what we need
Somebody gave us a watchman
watch him plant God's love seeds.
He gave us just what we asked for
We needed a leader above them all
No matter what you bring to this king's door.
He will open up his arms for more.

### **Stand**

You got to stand
and be counted
don't let the propaganda rule your world.

You got to stand
and be counted
don't let the propaganda rule your world

## You Ain't Cool

You ain't cool
I know you ain't
all the people that know you
don't know how fake you are
you ain't no star
a star would shine
no matter where they are
in the stenches of the trenches
eating chips for breakfast and
blunts for lunch.
We keep it crunch
like the backseat of the Mexican
an African born in America
But there's so much to this story
that I ain't been telling yah
from the corporate to the hip hop
I throw the confetti
manage ya projects
pour re me you with a machete
like spaghetti
you thought it was Italian
but its Chinese
I meet you half way
and bring you down to your knees.
You sneeze
I say bless you
you hold these
I undress you
caress you to a select few.

# The Many Faces of Mariama – The Fourth Letter

## **EM**

You think we don't know what you did
crossed eight mile when you was a kid
did what you had to do just to live
but then the story gets weird and
something's got to mother fucking give
they kept you safe in the hood
those boys in the neighborhood
but em we see now you took the good
contaminated our goods, you gave them pills and you would
put my boys in tutus and shit
got bizarre in a suit that was 3 sizes no fit
making my teeth grit cause my boys are gone
while I write this song my wrists I wanna slit
popsqaulies, got white donut residue on his lips
on a bike downtown go check him out when you dip
but they say you no longer hit them streets like you did
on 7 Mile, at the Hip Hop Shop with them misfits
critics say you're number one but really you number two
cause proof gave you your sound, your style and you ran with that too.
You gave us trailer park trash put purple pills in the hood
when the brothers was fine with blunted goods.
You gave us the clown look, took it and made us shook that's
laswunzout is still the laswunzout
cuz that silly shit you had them in made them boys clowns.

## Time

I am laying here
on the floor
Sobs choked back.
Life is robbing me
of that wonderful
I'm in Love feeling
I was feeling
just yesterday.

I realize that my cries
Can't bring that
feeling and that my
phone has stopped
ringing and now
My heart has
stopped singing
So, I just lay,

We've been through this
many times before
You and I... and so
When I cry
Sometimes now
Sometimes later
Wondering my heart
Couldn't he have
made her leave us
alone?

On the plane
landing now
I feel it
It's real it

## The Many Faces of Mariama – The Fourth Letter

hurts deep like
a muscle strain
and so I
travel home.

Home is empty
Couldn't he have
kept me feeling
so good, shouldn't
he have done what
I asked him to do?
Wake up Girl,
It isn't true.
What kind of love
Brings so much pain
Like dark angry
clouds bring so much
rain and sun and wind
and love bring skies
of blue?
Not understanding and
not knowing is worst
than Christmas time
Not snowing or faces
happy that are
not glowing or love
that you know is there
that you're not
showing.
What I want I can't
seem to have so
Instead of crying
I take a hot, soapy
bath and instead

of calling you
on the phone
I laugh, but my
heart is folding.

How can I get through
it this time?
This break up
this lover's quarrel
tomorrow?
We'll make up but
No I guess
I better wake up
that this won't be
true heals all
wounds
Someone
said and so I lay
awake in bed
counting seconds,
minutes, hours
while tears of showers
Engulf me.

Hopefully, hopefully
It will soon be over
control her urge
to love some more
my heart implores
my mind, wait on
time.
He will help you see
the light.
Time -

## The Many Faces of Mariama – The Fourth Letter

please come to me and
free me as I
desperately need
your presence as
the essence of love
has taken over my night.
And so, as always
I wait for day and
another like children
afraid of monsters
under beds my eyes
red already I steady
Wait.

I wait and ponder hoping
I could stop
thinking thinking
makes sadness
sinking deeper
darker like chocolate
cake

Bake something make
something write it
down but stop
letting the thoughts
of love gather round
your head instead
write it down
Has everyone felt
this empty?
Plenty of hurtness to share
if you haven't been
to this empty town.

## The Many Faces of Mariama – The Fourth Letter

I wouldn't wish this
sadness on anyone.
This madness is
really dumb.
It has put a hole in my heart.

Torn me apart in
pieces. Time
get the superglue
and wishes.
I'm just a pile of
broken dishes scattered
in the dark.

So as I clatter
walking round.
If things don't
seem to matter
right now, in
empty town,
Please understand
that my friend
Time
is holding my hand
and I pray my mind
will soon be sound.

## When I Fell in Love With You

I stand here before thee
to say that I adore thee
I declare to everyone out here
who is hearing me
this brother is so dear to me.
And then
he disappointed me.

You've hurt me
beyond compare
I didn't dare to live
I didn't dare to breathe
I wore my heart on my sleeve
and watched it bleed.

This fine, young beautiful thing
was an open all-night hang
who wasn't slick enough
to side track your bluff.

Instead of a treasure to hold on to
I was a temporary pleasure
for you to dump
your sperm.
You dumped your sperm.

I remember I felt like toxic waste
the pain was evident on my face
I couldn't erase the love I had
for you.
A charlatan whose
passion inspired sweat

## The Many Faces of Mariama – The Fourth Letter

I can still taste.

When I think about you today,
I turn seventeen all over again.
The tears run down my cheeks
as it if were only yesterday.

Because when you fall in love
you fall into a deep dark hole
Where no one can wipe
away your tears, no one
can comfort your fears
No one can console you
No one has control.

You see, They say you "fell"
in love because sometimes
you never get back up.

20 years later you may
haven't gotten on your feet
but you are bruised and
battered from the fall
and shattered from it all.

I was old and tired
at seventeen so,
when they say I feel I fell in love
I know exactly what they mean.

# The Many Faces of Mariama – The Fourth Letter

## Hitched

You used to call me
all the time before the two of you
got hitched.
This is before I became that
Quote,
"That stupid, needs-to-get-a life,
ignorant bitch".
He was fucking somebody else
and you felt a kinship to me
you see
he was fucking somebody else
on me, back in 93.
The father of my child,
now a husband to you and yours
of course,
You also had children by him but
he forced you to abort,
court days have passed
and he never showed up.
I remember you guys calling me
laughing and cuttin up.
I thought I could call on you
the same way I lended an ear
but now that you've got him
locked down, you fake like
I'm just a clown, perping like
"Homey, How can I be down?"
I was just wondering, if
yall got any spare change?
Out child is 12 now
and her clothes are growing with age.
"Don't call my house, you stupid

## The Many Faces of Mariama – The Fourth Letter

ignorant bitch" is what you said to
me and then I heard the phone go,
"Click".
I thought that we could talk
the way we talked when you were
tryin to understand why this man
wouldn't stop hurtin you and lyin.
I told you what I went through
and told you "everything will work
out fine"
Then you said, "Just call me
if you need anything" and
hung up the line.
I see now I can't talk to you
I gave you way too much credit.
I should have peeped your game
and saw just where you were headed.
Forget it.
I can't talk to him.
Last time I tried, he thought he was slick,
Your husband asked me for old time's sake
if I would suck his dick.
Think about that hitched bitch,
next time you call me ignorant.

## What?

What are we gonna do?
I'm getting so confused.
I wanna get into you,
But I gotta stay on my toes.
I got some inside news
some stuff nobody knows.
I'm gonna let it all go
as the reconciliation grows.
It so hard to love somebody
so easy to leave your lover
I'm not the one to talk
cuz I can't seem to get it
together.

## 360 Degrees

Just another day
360 Degrees
One more time
It don't mean nuthin
It don't mean a thang.
Like a grain of salt
I represent that judgement
It don't mean nuthin
to nobody
to act shady
you caress her ass
and then act crass
I can see through you
like a piece of glass.
I feel you like I feel jazz.
Ene, mini, miny, moe
Which one of you
gonna be my hoe?
That's a nigga for yah,
Don't know whose ass
he wants to tap
tomorrow he is here
to stay well, maybe
just for today.
Then , when he has
a burning pee, he feels
sorry for himself.
Always forgiven, you
always forgive him
mighty fast
like fast cash.
Don't care

## The Many Faces of Mariama – The Fourth Letter

where it came from
cause she needs new shoes
for her son.

## Sugar Daddy

Should I feel ashamed
that sometimes I can't pay my rent
that sometimes I get bent
off Smirnoff and juice
that I can get loose when
brothers start talking about those ends?
Should I?
Should I survive that blow
to my temple?
Simple Simon tried to leave me
blinded but, I rewinded that tape
so that would not be my misfortune
of course then,
Should I?
Should I disclose that my 9 to 5
really is being a ho?
I'm talkin about thigh highs and high heels
I'm talkin about lies we disguise
while doing business during business hours
Should I?
Should I stop looking for those child support payments
and stop thinking we can come to some sort
of arrangement and come to realize that
when the baby cries
I'm the one who has to go to the store
cause before.
I couldn't come to this conclusion
and I couldn't come out of the illusion
that my prince charming
was gonna come riding up in his caddy
and love me
and be my Sugar Daddy

# The Many Faces of Mariama – The Fourth Letter

be My Sugar Daddy
where is my Sugar Daddy
I see now he ain't thinking about me
he ain't thinking about me at all
My Sugar Daddy's at the Player's Ball
I realize there are other Hoes that need Clothes
so much competition being a Ho.

How many of us have made it sisters?
How many of us have made it to that apple pie?
Without one lie, without one blow
Without one lie, without one blow?
Without selling our thighs for cereal bowls?
Been undercover hoe and nobody knows?
More power to yah sisters!
More power to yah because you have to ask yourself
What would you do if your Sugar Daddy
didn't support you?

## Gotta Keep On Moving

Time is running out
many fears, many doubts.
Trying to find the best way out,
gonna rise, gonna shout.
Yah just gotta keep on moving!
Yah just gotta keep on grooving!
People falling by the way side,
don't know why, gonna cry.
Praying to the Lord every day,
gonna make it through, so we can fly.
Yah just gotta keep on moving!
Yah just gotta keep on grooving!
It's time to make a move right now
Don't look back to the past.
Ask if you don't know how
But make that move and make it fast.
Yah just gotta keep on moving!
Yah just gotta keep on grooving!
Nobody, Nobody, Nobody can stop us now!
Cause I got you and you got me,
as we tear down all our insecurities
We're gonna make it,
just watch and see
Pick your brother up off the ground
push him past the finish line.
Refuse to give it up now
cause if you do, you're gonna die.
Yah just gotta keep on moving!
Yah just gotta keep on grooving!

## The Many Faces of Mariama – The Fourth Letter

**I Need You Baby**

I need you baby,
is that ok to say?
Me being a woman, today,
steady getting paid.
Baby, I need you
not that couldn't breathe without you
because I could but, the air is not so tight.
When I breathe in your brown skin
I understand that woman
wanting that man.
That man who makes her feel whole
while she finds her individual soul.
Not being him. Not spending his money
or being funny or flaky, shaky right?
Not being called Dyke or Bitch cause
I walk and talk like I got a switch.
I still need you.
Not that I couldn't see without you
because I could but, my vision
isn't so blurry and I'm not in no hurry
to see anything with you standing next to me.
You straighten that abstract stigmatism
like a cataract disease that keeps me
from being such a whorish tease.
Baby, I need you.
I know I could walk without your steps
next to mine in sync but, I think
it's the harmony that brings me
to my knees to please you cause
you're beautiful.
And when you suck my breast,
you let me know the fuck is

## The Many Faces of Mariama – The Fourth Letter

gonna be good but, there is
gonna be some love made before
the fuck gets good.
It's floating in the air cause
my ass is warm with your hand smacking
it telling me my ass is yours
and the juice pours.
It overflows and nobody knows what it's
like but me cause this is my fantasy,
you are giving me.
Not the freaky, deaky, in-charge
spending ends, bar-hopping with friends,
lying, so much lying, about how
together somebody is.
In everybody's business.
It is a sickness you cure.
That allure is my need.
My fantasy to have love in reality.
It's so good, better than the high
or buzz, I had trying.
Trying to be something
that I wasn't.
I need you Baby, cause
I can be more of me
you make me whole.
Your soul is blessed and when
you say, "Yes",
I get undressed.
I confess, my willingness to
be what you need
to be the woman that you need.
I need you Baby,
cause you help me to be me.

## Could I Just Love You For Awhile?

Excuse me
But, could
I just love you
for a while?
You seem
to be so sweet.
May I massage
your feet?
Rub your back?
Not looking
for a one night stand.
Just an available man.
If it's not
too inconvenient,
could I
sit where
you sit?
Just wanna
smell your scent.
Not looking
for you to pay
my rent.
I have some
incense
and some wine.
No. That is not a line.
Don't you want
to unwind?
My fingers want
to smooth over
your temples.
Yes, it is

that simple.
Believe me.
I just want a man
to receive me.
I mean this.
I wish
I had a man
at my doorstep
when I get home.

**Stand Again**

We need to negotiate.
Our people out of your gates.
We need them at home to raise.
Their sons before it's too late.
Stand and be counted.
Don't let the propaganda rule your world.

## Endangered Species

Endangered species.
The black man.
So they lock you, cage you
enrage you, completely separate you
From the motherland.
and you wonder why
you so angry
nothing has made you
you made yourself.
And the wealth
that you chasing
is in the pockets
of another man.
You steady racing.
To get that income tax.
So you can flip that.
But now you in the red again.
You made your bed again.
Now yah sittin there,
wondering.
How yah gonna bring in the New Year
Everybody you started with last year ain't here.
Now you lookin like a crookin
somebody got shookin
I aint no rookie
So you know
somebody got tooken.
But my shadow is scared of me
But I paid my dues
Got a new pair of shoes
My people don't deliver good news.
I got the blues.

## Want to Believe

I know yah.
I know every little thing
about you Baby,
and when we fight
it gets so crazy.
I've been waiting
for you to recognize
all my complaints
and all my cries.
You walked away
and I turned around
to find you standing there
right in my face.
I want to chase
away your demons.
I hope and pray that
there's no scheming.
chorus: Want to believe
your apologies.
What does it mean
when you say those sweet things.
Want to believe
everything you say.
Cause baby right
you're making me want to stay.
I need yah.
You're the only whose been there for me
in times when
my back is up against the wall
and I feel like I'm drowning.
Quit clowning.
We're two adults

## The Many Faces of Mariama – The Fourth Letter

and we can't forget the spent
I need you to love me Baby
and not just pay the rent
and keep me bent.
What happened?
To the respect and the love
go find it.
Cause I got something for you Baby,
and I want you to get behind it.
chorus: Want to believe
your apologies.
What does it mean
when you say those sweet things.
Want to believe
everything you say.
Cause baby right
you're making me want to stay.

## I Got Naps

I got naps with my name on it.
Cause my man done put it on me.
He done made me feel so good.
That finger lickin good fly brutha
from the hood.

## 2 Lives

I know why we have 2 lives,
the blood runs dry on hands that bind.
I see all that you can see,
when now I live as not one, or two, but three.
So, hard to live in jungle Seuss said,
make them go to bed,
with rhymes in their head,
keep em moving back and forth on their feet
cuz its slush and snow and sleet in the "D".
You get fooled cuz you let yo guard down,
you feel like a clown here comes the boom now.
It's one and two and three now the clock strikes and
I can't take not one more pow.
Bang! somebody bit the dust,
love here has rust, dignity is a must.
Hard! I put my life on the line,
I got more than one rhyme, for everybody's crime.
I split my personality
because the world has gotten too hostile for me
and if you step to close to me
you will see that part of me.
Excuse me. You won't abuse me.
So, you see my bipolar in full effect
because your wreck has become my lack of check.
Connect. But don't forget
that simple gets complex
in a matter of secs.......

## Not Even a Glimpse of Love

The residue that you leave behind
as you climb like gun powder, they crowd you.
Want to see if there is a magic wand
or special brew that made you.
They want to see your blood dripping
with their tongue whipping unable to see life
through your eyes so they infatuate the world with lies.
Imagination so deep that even liars are afraid to creep.
No sleep. Yes sleep. Because where you are, I will never be.
How you smile crooked, they will never see me.
When you steal moments, I will hold peace.
Something you can never do or be.
Cause there is no peace on the streets.
So I fly high above and beyond what your lips bleed.
Indeed they watch above unable to catch
even a glimpse of love.
Not even a glimpse of love.
Sorry for your dud life.
Sorry you can't hurt mine.
Sorry you are full of lies.
Sorry you will die by the sharp of your tongue, young.

## When We Write History

When we write history,
they will know that Queens ran them streets,
we gave up with them beats to the hearts of the men they love.
When we write history,
they will say that we were Nefertiti and our seed travel through OUR veins,
not the men who were raped and played,
Our warrior men will see what we did good by them
while they were locked up during the War of 2011.
While they judge our daughters and our sons
for not having the strong to suffer the bullets holes
and hoes they call MOM.
MOM is what they say as she strays to reach
for that respect even though she strayed by the dead
she layed by the cursed she came.
Now yall know her name and you reek to blame.
Get outta ya hell that you live everyday
and know that we are the most powerful people in Mankind Creed.
Once I tell them that I run the world, they will swirl their bullets will soar.
Once I tell the people to raise up its over cuz I built them up,
I built them up and made them strong
and told them tomorrow the day is long
and you will follow me out of darkness
cuz while you was locked up I did my damnest.
Kept yo baby fed and kept him sleep in bed and even made him President.
So stop yo complain and be my man
understand what you are is what I am.....

## I Am Found Where Love Is

How am I
supposed to
Make it through
I loved you
I won't hold
Onto something
That's so blue
What can I
Say to you
make you stop
act a fool
wanna school
you on loving
me but
that's not what
I should do
Cuz its over
I'm done
Gotta run,
Higher than the sun
Taller than the hill
Deeper than the sea
You won't find me
You won't find me
Cuz I'm found
Where love is
You see me
Minding my biz
And I'm round the way
Where love is
You find me

Where love is

## Got To Be Strong

Never thought that I would say goodbye
Grabbed my things now I got to ride
People look at me and they ask why
No longer want to be the one to cry
Want to find my way
So I cannot stay
Got to be the strong

## Never Told Me Why

And they never told me why
why I couldn't make it out.
All I wanted was my life
but I didn't know what
life was all about.
What life is about
What life is about
What life is about.
Now the struggle is so real
while you stand there watching me.
You don't even want to deal
cuz you're so caught up in your own misery.
What life is about
What life is about
What life is about.

# The Many Faces of Mariama – The Fourth Letter

## A Poem to the Africans Born In America

We kill for shoes, But we have shoes
What if we walked in other's shoes
That they don't have, and then we laugh
But then we both have the blues
Are water runs, For them no water comes
There is no food, Just political rule
Who is the fool?
For them there is no school, Our children rule
But we have school
We have everything, Except what life should bring
They have smiles for miles, We have guns and knives
we have false cries, and bloody skies
their heart is pure, our heart manure
we can't relate, the time is late
no time to thank, our mother's back
we just attack, and smoke our crack
they know the love, something we know nothing of
their love fits like a glove, it was once was
for us the time is late, we can't escape
our greed and need, to have more than we sow
our seed is dry, now no water comes
to those who don't love, their mother's throne
Who can't call their house a home
Who don't know their father's face, or name, or race.
In case, you didn't see
Their faces look like you and me.

## The Many Faces of Mariama – The Fourth Letter

Thank you to all of my friends and family. You have always believed in me. Thank you to the Tall family and Mr. Tall. Thank you to my children and my mother and father. At the end of the day, you are all that matters to me. Thank you to all those who love Hip Hop and won't let it die.
Rhythma De'twa

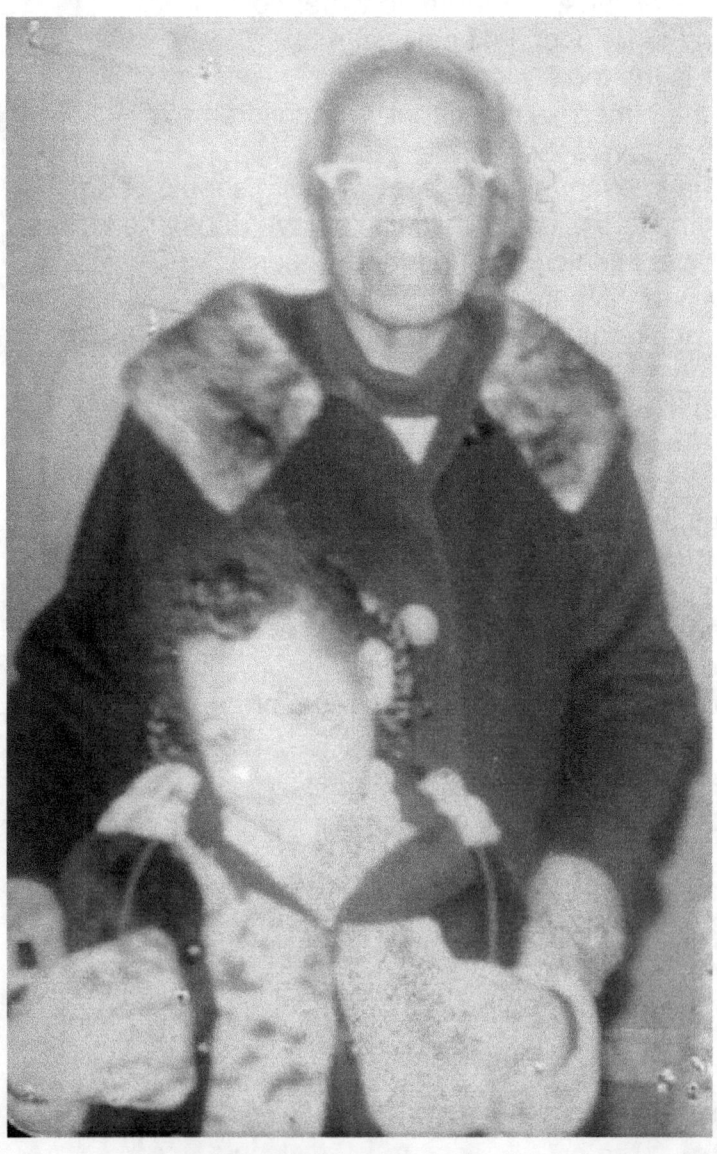

# The Many Faces of Mariama – The Fourth Letter

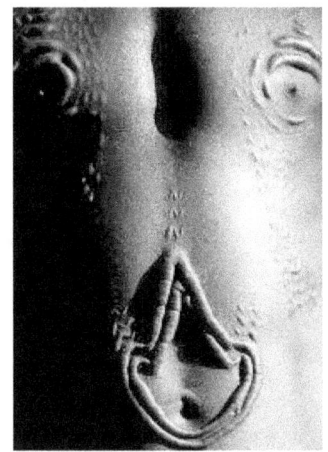